The Persistence of Rivers

an essay on moving water

Winner of The Florida Review's Jeanne Leiby Award

Alison Townsend

BURROW PRESS | ORLANDO, FL

Published by Burrow Press, in partnership with *The Florida Review*'s Jeanne Leiby Award.

POD Edition. © Alison Townsend, 2017. All rights reserved.

Cover Art: "Big Cottonwood Canyon in September"
Pastels on sanded paper © Jennifer Worsley

Cover and book design: Liesl Swogger

Jeanne Leiby Award Series Editor: Susan Fallows
The Florida Review Editor: Lisa Roney

ISBN: 978-1-941681-83-1
eISBN: 978-1-941681-84-8
LCCN: 2016957430

Distributed by Itasca Books
orders@itascabooks.com

Burrow Press
PO Box 533709
Orlando, FL 32853
burrowpress.com

Jeanne Leiby Award

In Memory of Jeanne Leiby, 1964-2011

As editor of *The Florida Review* from 2004 to 2007, Jeanne breathed new life into the University of Central Florida's literary journal. She brought graphic narratives to *TFR*, initiated the journal's first web site, published the special 30th anniversary issue, and brought together a smart team of graduate students and taught them to be editors.

Established after Jeanne's death in 2011, the award commemorates her commitment to writing and publishing by offering the winner both a monetary award and publication in the form of a chapbook.

Special thanks to this year's judge, Vanessa Blakeslee.

Patrons of the Jeanne Leiby Award

Pat and Jim Leiby
Bennet Heart and Anne Leiby
Rob Raff
Anonymous

I. The Wisconsin River, Mazomanie, Wisconsin 7

II. The Perkiomen River, Pennsburg, Pennsylvania 11

III. The Perkiomen, Again 15

IV. Styx-Hudson 25

V. Titicus River, North Salem, New York 27

VI. Day Lily: Interlude with
Colonial House and Stream 39

VII. Marys River, Wren, Oregon 49

VIII. The Yahara River,
Pleasant Springs Township, Wisconsin 67

All water has a perfect memory and is forever trying to get back to where it was.

– TONI MORRISON

I. The Wisconsin River, Mazomanie, Wisconsin

I'm sitting on the front porch of a cabin on the banks of the Wisconsin River, watching the morning hours slide past on the river's silver back. The river is somehow still and moving at the same time, as wide rivers often appear to be, its surface reflecting a blurred picture of trees, sandy islands, and sky that, if I stare at them all long enough, become a dream the river is having about itself. What is it like to reflect things that way, I wonder, one element of this world showing others to themselves? I read a book once in which the author posited that water possesses consciousness. This morning, staring early into river light, it is easy to believe the river is aware. It glimmers back at me through the mist, illuminating everything the way memory sometimes does—the present infused by the past—as if from down a long blue corridor where we suddenly recognize ourselves. "Sometimes there are rivers," I wrote many years ago to a man I once loved, "that tell you who you are." I was writing about a tangled stream that rushed out of Big Santa Anita Canyon in the San Gabriel Mountains, as different a channel of water from this placid-looking river as you can imagine. And yet it too reflected the landscape around it. It too dreamed.

The Persistence of Rivers

The best thing about the cabin where I now sit, watching the river, is the fact that, in the impromptu, hodge-podge manner of cabins everywhere, the bed is on the front porch. Because of this, the river is the first thing you see in the morning and the last thing you see before you go to sleep. Even during the night, when I wake up, I can see it out there, sliding silently by on its watery business, shining with the dull glow of old silver, reflecting clouds, stars, moonlight. I love being able to sit up in bed in the morning with my journal, a mug of tea, and three pillows at my back, watching the river to see what it has to say, a landscape of possibility opening before me.

I have a friend who grew up along this river, and I've found myself thinking of her while I've been here, imagining her as a girl on the banks of these waters. Though I was raised in landscapes where mountains—or at least hills—served as the primary physical and emotional frames of reference, I can see how living beside a river such as this would imprint one with both stillness and fluidity, the ability to be in motion and to be both calm and aware of being in motion at the same time. Although the Wisconsin is different—and bigger than—rivers I have known well, watching it takes me back to my own origins in water. I think of rivers that began me, like the Perkiomen in eastern Pennsylvania, rivers that raised me and helped me endure, like the Titicus in rural New York

State, rivers that healed me, giving me back to myself, like the Marys River in western Oregon, and finally, rivers that have taught me something I didn't know about myself, such as the Yahara in Wisconsin.

I think of larger rivers too. The Schuylkill River defined my early girlhood, marking the way in from the country to my grandmother's house in Philadelphia, single sculls skimming across its surface like birds, exactly like the print of a Thomas Eakins painting that hung in our living room. I think of the Hudson, which my family crossed over on the Tappan Zee Bridge as if it were the River Styx, moving to New York State at the beginning of the end of my mother's life. I think of the Rogue in western Oregon, where I hiked along wild and precipitous banks in my early thirties, still fragile from a nervous breakdown and weeping at the sight of salmon as they leapt again and again up the waterfall, their battered silver bodies driven by instinct to return, against all obstacles, to the home stream. To have seen such a thing even once is to have stood in the presence of miracles, filled with what, in a book my aunt gave me after my mother died, Rachel Carson so aptly describes as "a sense of wonder."

Just listing the names of the rivers, large and small, I have known or spent time beside, I realize that, though I think of myself as a "mountains and ocean" person, my life has, in fact, been laced through by rivers, as surely as if I had been born with their courses inscribed in my palm. Large and small, they have defined me in the same way they define a landscape, cutting through it, changing it, determining what happens on its shores. An American Studies major in college, I once spent an entire semester studying the role rivers played in the settlement of this country. But I had not thought about what rivers might mean on a personal level, or about what those intimate lanes of water some might call creeks or streams had to tell me about how we come to be who we are. It is as if their bright music was so much a part of my life that I hardly even heard it unless I stopped to listen. But even now, walking beside a creek or stream, I stop and incline my head, as if hearing a familiar language in its swirls, splashes, and riffles. If I just listen hard enough, I think to myself, it will tell me how to live in this world. But of course I never understand its message completely.

II. The Perkiomen River, Pennsburg, Pennsylvania

I am not romanticizing or being poetic when I say that the sound of running water began me. It was the first sound I knew, its ripple and babble present in my consciousness before I ever saw it, for my parents brought me as an infant to an old fieldstone farmhouse right on the banks of the Perkiomen River. We only lived there for the first few years of my life before we moved to another old house, Wild Run Farm, the true Eden of my childhood. But perhaps because I had a brush with death during those first years, I have a number of crystalline memories of The Old House, as we came to call it. Some are snapshots, involving my parents' faces, or glimpses, like Vermeer paintings, into rooms. But most of my memories involve the Perkiomen, which tumbled beside our house in ceaseless conversation with itself and the land. Much more than just a background sound, the river was a kind of voice, one that lulled me, perhaps because, as my father told me years later, he and my mother walked beside it nearly every day, me strapped against one of them in a Snugli baby carrier. "It always calmed you down," my father said. "It was like a lullaby." And how could it be anything else? The sound of running water, both echo and source, is a reminder of the rivers flowing in of all our mothers' bodies.

The room where I slept faced the river and, at least in the summer, my mother pushed my crib right up against the window so I could look out across the water. Though I had no name for the river, I thought of it as a kind of liquid path one could follow forever, to the fields beyond, where a nearby farmer's Holsteins grazed, tiny figures in an enormous green landscape under puffy clouds. My mother, who had an extraordinary affinity with animals, fed eastern bluebirds (this was the early 1950s, before DDT brought the species to near extinction) from that window. The sound of her voice calling, "Here bluebird, here bluebird," wove itself into the sound of running water with grace and authority, making an impression on me. In the family mythology, "bluebird" was the first word I uttered. I wish I could claim to remember that moment when I matched the bird with sky on its shoulders to its name, but of course I do not. I question the myth instead, wondering if, like so many family stories, that is how things really happened or how we wish they had.

But I have no doubt about the sound of the Perkiomen and how it imprinted me with its velvety murmur as it tumbled over amber-colored stones, sorting them by size so neatly they seemed arranged at its bottom like a beautiful mosaic. I liked to dabble in the water, as all children do, watching the current swirl around my starfish hands, turning over stones. Moving even a single pebble altered the river slightly, though it did not stop its flow. I have a vivid image of crouching at the water's edge with my father, who liked to sit beside the river, watching as it sinuously and effortlessly rearranged itself. Though I had no idea we were engaged in contemplation, I learned something about its power and value in those moments beside moving water.

I learned something similar from my mother as I stood in the crib beside the window. In my first memory, I look out over the river and the fields. I have arranged all my stuffed animals along the window side of the crib so they also look out over the river. Holding myself up by the bars of the crib, I stare out over the scene. The river is a sparkling line beneath me, one that seems to demarcate the world of the house, my parents, my mother's twenty beloved cats, from the world beyond. I watch the cows move slowly across the green grass. I watch the clouds. I watch the river, laid down before me, and then look up, to see its ripples reflected on the walls and ceiling in waves of moving light. As I watch, something happens. There is a *here*—a place I know well, one that forms the limits of my small world—and a *there*—places I know nothing about, enormous realms waiting to be discovered. The vista seems endless and I feel as if I could gaze at it forever, the stuffed Scottie dog and panda watching beside me. I am alone, but I am not lonely. All I want to do is look.

That experience at the window is something I've thought about during times when loneliness has been my predominant emotion. If, as some psychologists say, our first memories are important templates, offering us patterns by which we can better understand our lives, mine is a good one, given to me by people who, each in their own way, understood the importance of looking. Writer Barry Lopez amplifies the idea of such a psychic imprint when he recalls something Wallace Stegner once said about place: "Whatever landscape a child is exposed to early on, that will be the sort of gauze through which he or she will see all the world afterward." Lopez enlarges on this experience by describing it as "emotional sight, not strictly a physical thing," which makes sense to me. But I would add sound. For the background of my beginning is alive with the murmur of running water. The Perkiomen purls smoothly over stones, the landscape around it illuminated by streamlight, by water into which many voices seem to have fallen and out of which many voices seem to emerge; it is a thread of silver pulled through my first years, my parents' gift to me, everything since stitched with the memory of its sound.

III. The Perkiomen, Again

We left the house beside the river in 1955 and moved to Wild Run Farm. I almost died that spring, ill with a fever of unknown origin that sent me to Children's Hospital of Philadelphia for a number of weeks, so I have no memory of leaving the Old House or arriving at Wild Run Farm. Instead, a number of indelible images of the hospital are burnt into my being, primary colors outlined in shimmering bursts of light, as if illuminated by the popping flashbulbs of that era. In one, my parents try to distract me with a bowl of chocolate ice cream while the pediatrician makes a venous cutdown into my left ankle for an IV. In another, I awake at night in a white iron crib to see my mother leaning over me like an angel. I am burning up, then packed in ice. They are changing the IV in my ankle. I fall asleep, watching the gold of city lights, no sound of the river anywhere. Finally, I am on the mend, "helping" a nurse fold a little pile of nubbly, white, institutional washcloths, wondering why I am not yet well enough to eat Easter candy.

And then I am home, though in a strange place, one I do not recognize, waking up from an afternoon nap in my father's study to the sound of a pine branch scraping the window. It's a cloudy day and everything seems grey, pearlized by some trick of early summer light. Nothing stirs after the pine branch falls still, and, as I look out the window, I am aware of something missing. The river is not there. I cannot hear its music or see the distant cows grazing on the horizon against which I have always measured my small days. I am filled with a silence so immense that I seem to blur around the edges, running into it, merging with it, as if I have been absorbed in its fabric. I don't know yet, of course, that this particular country silence, this green world, dreaming deeply around me, is something I'll seek my entire life when living in other, noisier places. All I know is I am held by it, adapting to its shape, as water fills a pitcher, and this silence fills me with something that, though I have no name for it, I recognize as peace.

But the sound of running water has vanished, as mysteriously as The Old House. At various points throughout my childhood, my father will explain to me that we had to move away from The Old House because the land where it stood was flooded to make Green Lane Reservoir. Did that mean, as I reasoned at the time, The Old House had drowned and was covered in water? Did fish swim through the windows where my mother had sung and we both had watched the bluebirds? I imagined the house, ghostly white beneath the water, its walls wavering and shining. When we drove over the causeway across the reservoir into Pennsburg village, I gazed out across the water, looking for signs of The Old House, the stone chimney perhaps, or the tip of the red roof sticking out of the water. I saw only the flat expanse of shining water that seemed to stretch on without end, vaguely ominous in its vastness.

One summer—during a drought so bad it brought the neighbors up the road to our door with jars for water when their well went dry—the reservoir's levels dropped so low the crumbled foundations of houses appeared like beached ships on the dry lakebed. Was one of them The Old House? Was that all that was left of it? The fading outlines on the striated shoreline haunted me. *Someone lived there once*, I thought to myself, looking at the foundations revealed by the drought as we drove past. *Someone lived there and it was us.* Where had the river that ran beneath my window gone? Where were the bluebirds? Where was the house I did not remember leaving? Regarding it all as we passed in the car, I understood something of the meaning of time passing.

Fortunately, the river, which twisted and turned around Pennsburg and through Montgomery County, wasn't far away at all, but just down the road from Wild Run Farm. It wasn't close enough that my brother, sister, and I could play in it unsupervised. But on hot summer afternoons we often walked down to it, accompanied by my mother and our corgi-beagle pups, Megan and Tina. The road was dirt, hot and white, little puffs of dust erupting beneath our feet. But the river, which ran beneath a chunky, moss-covered WPA-era bridge at the bottom of the road, was cool and sweet, a million shifting strands of silver twirled together, then pressed flat in a rippled bolt of water. Sometimes we stood on the bridge, playing Poohsticks or fashioning small boats from leaves. We'd drop them into the water on one side, then race across the bridge, looking not so much for whose was ahead but for where they were going. Resting my cheek against the rough aggregate of the bridge, tracing my fingers idly across its surface, I'd stare down into the river, wondering where it led, until I lost sight of my boat around a bend in its leafy shadows.

Other times we slid like otters down the steep path at one end of the bridge. The river ran wide and shallow here, the color of pale tea, paved with many rocks, like a kind of underwater, cobbled road. But it was good for wading, and we spent hours beside its glancing, golden light, building fairy houses and miniature villages, or exploring the shallows in cut-out Keds my practical mother turned into summer sandals. Poking around, without apparent purpose, we were pulled into the river's reverie, held in a daydream that unfurled before us, lulling in its movement. My mother sketched. We splashed in the river's riffles and pools, feeling the gentle tug of its current. I stretched full length on the bank toward it, trying to lap from the river as I imagined an otter might. The water, which was cold and clear, tasted of minerals. Bracing and ancient, it seemed like water from another time. I lapped quickly, then plunged my face into the river, its current brushing my skin like invisible hands that pulled me away from the solidity of the green bank, my mother and her pastels, the sounds of my brother and sister playing.

Lifting my face from the water, I stared down into it. The otter was gone and someone, who looked like me but wasn't quite, floated among the trees and clouds and leaves, reflected among them like a peculiar island, everything still and moving at the same time. As I watched, something twisted and turned in my body and seemed to float away, merging with water and sky. I felt tiny, small as one of the flecks of pollen that floated like gold dust on the river's surface. What was an "I" anyway? What did it mean that I was alive, human, a girl with wet braids, trailing her fingers in the water until they were wrinkled and pale? The feeling, which I could never summon voluntarily, made me feel thin and insubstantial as petals of the trilliums we looked for near the river in the spring. It was defined by such a heightened sense of reality that I felt unreal. It came upon me as a waking dream, both thrilling and disconcerting. I rode the feeling out in waves, until it dissolved around the edges, like a fraying maple leaf caught under a stone and worn away by the water, until only the skeleton remained and I was returned to who I was, an ordinary girl, the river running beside me.

The pups loved the water, too, and bounced and splashed beside us, until the day Tina, the one with orange eyebrows who made my mother laugh, was struck and killed by a blue pickup as it roared past on the road. I still remember my mother holding the dead puppy in her arms and saying over and over, "He didn't stop. He didn't even stop." We returned to the house, and, after my mother dug a hole at the edge of the hayfield, I helped her wrap Tina in a length of blue calico. She let Megan sniff at her before lowering Tina's still-warm body into the ground. My mother was crying so hard she could barely speak, snot running down her face the way it ran down mine when I cried. It was as if the river had broken inside her. In that moment, I realized that my mother, who had seemed invincible, couldn't do everything. As I sat there in the sweet-scented field beside my mother, the river seemed to well up inside my chest too, and I felt an enormous tenderness for her. Did I place my small hand over her work-roughened one, or did she reach out and take mine as we walked back to the house?

We didn't walk down to the river for many weeks after that, and when we did, it was with a sense of caution and sadness. Megan was tethered to us by a bright red leash and my mother insisted on walking on the outside. But the road, rarely traveled by anyone but the mailman, was silent. When we got to the river, it seemed darker and sadder, tinted copper in the long light and late summer shadows, running and running and running. Dropping my stick in the water that day, hanging over the edge of the bridge, all I could think of was Tina, there and then not there, and the sound of my mother's weeping.

If the river was sweet relief in the humid Pennsylvania summers, in the winter it was a brilliantly etched, crystalline world of blue and white, an illustration from *The Snow Queen*. A number of times during the winter, and always on a weekend, when my father was home, my parents took us on excursions to the river. On those days, instead of walking down the road, we cut through the woods across from our house and followed a tiny stream downhill to the river. Frozen over, rimmed with ice in fantastic formations, the stream was a world of its own, one where blue caves shimmered, crystal chandeliers tinkled and delicate goblets shone, all at the edge of water so dark it was almost black.

Fascinated by the miniature worlds and snow palaces the ice revealed, I ran ahead, entranced by what I saw, looking and looking. Ever the scientist, my biochemist father was probably explaining something about how the ice formed. But my mother was quiet, looking closely as well, holding his hand in her red-mittened one. Everything sparkled, spangled with light. The stream was a bright voice, chittering beneath its frozen surface, then rushing downhill to join the river's larger one, where we stood for a while, awed by its winter velocity and power. Watching the freezing water surge past, I hugged my mother close, steadying myself against the familiar contours of her body, amazed that this was the same river I had stuck my face into the summer before. How did things change so quickly and so completely, from one season to another? Did I change that way too? Did anything stay the same?

We left Wild Run Farm and the Perkiomen just a few years later, when I was nine. My mother was already dying of breast cancer, though it had not been confirmed, and my father had been offered a new job at Geigy Pharmaceuticals. The position was so much better than the one he held at Merck, in Philadelphia, that (as he told me years later) he couldn't afford not to take it. With no understanding of what it means to leave a place that has made you who you are, my brother and sister and I were caught up in the excitement of the move, thrilled by the van with a painting of the Mayflower on its side and the enormous boxes the friendly movers gave us to play in. But as we drove away on a hot August afternoon, leaving Wild Run Farm empty and echoing, I turned briefly and reached over the back seat to comfort my Dutch rabbit, Babe. As I stroked her soft brown and white fur, I gazed down the road behind us, filled with a curious feeling. It didn't last long, but it was there, the shape of loss settling inside me, a quiet presence that would inhabit me forever. I watched dust glitter in the sunlight before it settled behind the car. I watched the dark green hollow at the end of the tunnel of trees, where the river ran, going about its silvery business, oblivious to our departure.

As the car rolled forward, I looked back. "*Perkiomen, Perkiomen,*" I said to myself, turning the word, which was then—and always—beautiful to me, over and over in my head, as if to engrave the sound of running water in my consciousness. I wanted to tell my father to stop the car. But we turned the curve onto Bowers Mill Road, and Wild Run Farm and the lane down to the river were gone. I would not see either again for nearly forty years, until the summer my father died, when I'd lean over the WPA bridge—which, astonishingly, stood firm, as if no time had passed—my tears falling into the water, like minnows loosed in the home stream. As I traced my fingers across the pebbled surface of the bridge and gazed into the amber water, everything was exactly the same. And everything was different—and haunted—as is the way of things when one revisits the Ur-places of childhood. I was not sure it was good I had returned, except that I was reassured it was all still there, in a kind of parallel world, another family with three young children living at Wild Run Farm, the river running on without me. I did not stay long that day, sensing my time there had passed, as it had for others before me, swift as creek water gurgling over stones with a bright, glancing sound I will always remember. *Perkiomen, Perkiomen.* Even now, the word has the power of a spell or incantation. Like a secret code only my brother and sister and I know, when repeated over and over, it evokes a vanished world. "I bring you some water lost in your memory," says poet Patrice de La Tour du Pin. "Follow me to the spring and find its secret." The Perkiomen holds mine. I will never plumb its secrets completely.

IV. Styx-Hudson

We crossed the Hudson River to get to our new home in New York State. We crossed it and I did not look back. It was the biggest river I had seen after the Delaware, and, as we sped along the dizzying grey lanes of the Tappan Zee Bridge, I held my breath, looking out the car window at the blue vastness that swirled below, afraid the bridge cables might snap and we'd plummet to our deaths. That winter, I'd feel the stiff winds blow down the Hudson in Dobbs Ferry, the town in lower Westchester County where we lived for a year, but the river itself was mostly an invisible presence, its cold breath huffing over us like that of a large, dangerous animal. A few years later, Pete Seeger would spearhead a famous—and very successful—effort to clean it up. The tall ships would sail up the Hudson during the Bicentennial, their white sails billowing out so beautifully that I wept, a pride I rarely feel in my country welling up within. Decades later, when birds clogged its engines, a plane would land in it, all the passengers surviving, as if descending over liquid tarmac. I myself wrote a report on the river in eighth grade for my New York State history class, marveling at the role it had played in shaping the place where I lived. It's a beautiful river. But for me the Hudson was also the River Styx. My mother died. My father remarried just six months later, trying to fill a loss that tore him open like a shot to the heart. I felt the Hudson's cold breath on the nape of my neck, closer and closer. It caught me. It held me in its cold arms. It woke me, screaming and inconsolable, in the middle of the night. It swept me under. River of death. River of darkness and dread. River of sorrow. River from which, having crossed over it into another country, one does not return. The Styx-Hudson washed childhood away.

V. Titicus River, North Salem, New York

I did not live in close proximity to a river again until I was twelve, when my family, which now included two stepbrothers, moved to North Salem, a small town in northeastern Westchester County, where I spent the rest of my girlhood. There are many stereotypes about Westchester, all of which irritate me, for none describe the town where I grew up. Located fifty-five miles from New York City, at about the farthest distance commuter fathers like my own were willing to travel by train, North Salem was pocked here and there with orchards, small dairies, and horse farms. Densely green and rural, the town seemed to float in its own pocket of time, slightly out of step with the rest of the world. There were wealthy properties in the town, yes, inhabited during holiday weekends and summers by small influxes of what we scornfully referred to as "city people." But the kids I attended school with were the children of ordinary people—mechanics, nurses, farmers, the local postmistress. The North Salem I knew was a place characterized by its lakes, rushing streams, wooded hills, fertile valleys, beautiful views—and a river, the Titicus, which wound through the township like a snip of blue ribbon.

The Persistence of Rivers

Titicus, Titicus. The name, like so many in the Northeast, is an abbreviated form of an ancient Indian word, *Mughtiticoos*, which translates as "place without trees." But when I say Titicus, the word unfolds in my mouth like a rare spice, its spiky consonants punctuating my breath. I see the river where it ran under the bridge at the end of our road, dark copper as a tarnished penny, shaded on each side by dense stands of oaks and sugar maples. Its banks were steep there, and the river ran swiftly, headed toward a small dam and a waterfall just downstream. I crossed the bridge twice a day, walking the half mile between the big white house where we lived at the top of the hill, in one of the town's original homesteads, and the school bus stop at the flagpole on the triangular village green.

The bridge was high and the river, at least at first, seemed to me dark and secretive, as filled with mystery as the inside of my rapidly changing body. Though I'd often stop and gaze down into the river, something about it—its shadows, its depth, its pace as it quickened toward the waterfall—made me anxious. If I stared down into the dark, honey-colored water for too long, I began to feel a kind of vertigo that made me pull back, afraid of falling, or perhaps even climbing over the bridge to see if, in some weird test of fate, I could fly. Once, while I was in the grip of one of those feelings, a fisherman startled me, stepping out from behind the trees like a figure hidden in one of Currier and Ives' puzzle pictures. Native brown trout ran in the Titicus, which was also stocked with rainbows, so it wasn't uncommon to see fishermen from out of town along the river, silent sentinels watching the water run by, waiting for a tug on their lines.

But this one spoke to me, asking me about myself in a manner that suggested I was an adult, not a young teen with dots of Clearasil on my face and a humiliating tendency to turn scarlet whenever I opened my mouth. The fisherman had brown eyes and hair almost the color of the river and carried an old-fashioned creel and willow basket. He asked me about the town, the stream, what I was doing there, and seemed genuinely interested in my responses. As we spoke, something I never felt before seemed to catch and flutter between us. I felt as gripped by his brown gaze as I had been by the river a moment before. I don't believe the fisherman meant me any harm. In retrospect, he seems one of those adults who possess the rare gift of treating children as seriously as they deserve to be taken. But his attention cast a spell over me. Something about the encounter unnerved me, and I finally burst out with an inelegant, "Well, I have to go now," and ran up the road, clutching my heavy, blue introductory French textbook against my chest.

The Persistence of Rivers

As I moved from the green chill—delicious to step into in summer—that always hung over the bridge and into the sunlight of open fields and stone walls that had stood for two hundred years, I had the distinct sense something momentous had happened. I'd had an experience I didn't even begin to understand and somehow it all had to do with the river, which both mesmerized and frightened me. The river was just doing what rivers do, running with its braided amber colors through the dappled light, but it provided me with a reference point in the landscape, one whose swirls and shadows showed me things I couldn't articulate. I didn't tell anyone about meeting the fisherman. But I thought about him for a long time that night as I lay in bed, remembering how the rhythm of the Titicus—echoing under the bridge until it seemed to vibrate up through my entire body—had seeped into my cells when he spoke.

If the river was shadowed at the end of our road, it wound, true to its Indian name, through the mostly sunny fields that surrounded our neighbors' houses. One of these neighbors was a family of freckle-faced boys, the Feeners, who dove into the river from a rope swing in their backyard, swaying back and forth across the deep coffee-and-cream-colored water before letting go with a whoop. My brothers swam there on a regular basis, but it was definitely boys' territory, and I never thought—or wanted—to join them. I wasn't the strongest swimmer at the time, and the thought of flinging myself out across the river on the rope terrified me nearly as much as the oldest of the freckled boys, who was in my class and so good in algebra, which I was failing, that he was rumored to be some kind of genius. He interested me, in an abstract kind of way. But it did not occur to me to try and infiltrate this realm, where boys' pale bodies swayed, dappled with river light and tree shadows, strange as another species, before disappearing into the swiftly moving water.

But the next neighbor up the road had a daughter, Nan, just a year younger than me. Walking back and forth to the bus stop every day, Nan and I became friends. Drawn together at first by our love of horses, our attention turned gradually, as subtly as the sunflowers lining the edge of her mother's garden leaning into the sun, toward the idea of boys. Nan's parents' place had a farm pond, a small ox-bow really, which the river ran through at one end. Nan and I paddled in the pond on hot summer days, stepping gingerly through the muck toward deeper water, the boys' shouts echoing from just around the bend. Although we were secretly fascinated by them, and vaguely aware, through the scrim of trees that separated our world from theirs, that they were trying to impress us, we had no real desire to join them. Ponds are private places, and our pond, shining caramel in the sun, felt like a separate country, one where we could be completely ourselves. We did strange little dances in the water to the faint sounds of my transistor radio, 77-WABC echoing down from the banks where we'd spread our towels, or we dared one another to pull down the tops of our bathing suits, letting the shimmering water, glittering with mica, stream down over our nearly nonexistent breasts.

Nan and I tended, at least at first, to confine our swims to the placid, unruffled pond. But if we swam to the edge, where the river ran through, we could feel the irresistible pull of its current, trying to draw us downstream. Holding on to the bank, we'd stretch out full length, delighting in the tug and sway of the water moving us, even as we stayed in place. Only our hair, which we both wore long (though mine was straight and hers was curly), surrendered to the current, streaming out behind us like liquid capes, caressing our backs and shoulders as lightly as river grasses. The pleasure of the moment lay entirely in the possibility of letting go, of being almost swept away. Occasionally, one of us would lose our grip, at which point we'd cling to the other, laughing and shrieking, the stillness broken as we wrestled like the girls we still were.

If the area downriver from the pond, dominated by the boys' exploits, felt off-limits to us, the area upriver, with its entrancing twists and turns, pulled at our attention, exciting our curiosity about what lay around the next bend. On languid summer afternoons, when everything seemed to stand still, Nan and I pushed her parents' old rowboat, its blue paint chipped and fading, into the pond. After some maneuvering, we headed upriver, in the direction of Connecticut, where the Titicus begins. Connecticut wasn't far away; I grocery-shopped with my father at the Grand Union in Ridgefield every Saturday morning. But small towns are worlds unto themselves, and Nan and I were thrilled with the idea that we were, as we called it, "rowing to Connecticut."

Once we left the pond, the water ran clearer and deeper. Gazing down through it, we could see large, flat rocks, coated in silt and impossibly slippery to stand on. Every now and then, the speckled side of a trout flashed past. Jewel and pickerel weed, bulrushes, thistles, and milkweed crowded the banks in a kind of low hedge that made us feel both cut off and sheltered from everything around us. We rowed, sometimes in tandem, our damp thighs brushing against one another as we sat, crammed into the splintery seat, and sometimes singly, the girl who wasn't rowing seated in the prow of the boat like a figurehead, calling out what landmarks lay ahead. Every now and then, when we got hot, one of us would lower ourselves into the water and hang on to the back of the boat as the other rowed, savoring the flow of the river as it sluiced around us, stroking us with cool, invisible hands. When I was the one being towed, I'd close my eyes, tilt my face up to the sun, and give myself over to the moment in a way it is only possible to do when you are still half-child, without any conscious thought of what you are doing. The oars creaked. The water streamed past my body. If I opened my eyes, I could see Nan, looking at me as she rowed, her upper lip beaded with tiny pearls of sweat, her damp hair curling around her shoulders. We could spend an entire afternoon that way.

On one of these excursions up the river I had an experience I have never been able to understand, perhaps because I cannot remember it completely, time and the river having silted it over so only the outlines of it linger, like those broad, flat rocks at the bottom. The same kind of rocks jutted out from the banks at one bend in the river. They formed natural sunning spots for bullfrogs, which often startled us with their galumphing splash, or yellow-and-red-striped painted turtles, which slid into the water silently, with a grace belied by their awkward-looking bodies. It was on these rocks that something happened. We met a boy, not someone we knew, coming downriver in a boat like ours, the channel narrow enough we had to pull aside to let him pass. Or was the boy already there, alone, without a boat, fishing or swimming? Or was I alone in the blue boat,

Nan left behind for some reason? I dip my net again and again into memory's water, but cannot come up with a completely clear picture.

What I do remember is the boy—strong, slender, tanned, his brownish hair bleached blond by summer—and me standing there on the rocks beside him, talking to him, after he'd helped me from the boat, his fingers firm and cool against mine. We weren't flirting exactly. But something about him exerted a mysterious pull, real yet invisible as the currents of the river itself. He seemed outlined in light and I felt on unexpectedly equal ground with him. If I had to give it a name now, I might call the feeling that infused those moments on the rocks with the boy *yearning*. I yearned for the boy as I yearned for what lay around the next bend of the river. I longed for him as I longed to let myself go in the water's pull. I ached for him, as we can only ache for things we have not yet experienced but which our bodies somehow already know.

And that, really, was all that happened. Some sort of mysterious exchange or understanding passed between us, as we stood there on the rocks together, the river swishing past. Then I stepped back into the boat or slipped back into the water, and returned to Nan, changed from who I had been. "What was that about?" I remember her asking. "Nothing, it was nothing," I said, wanting only to be alone with the feeling, away from what felt like her poking and prodding. Instead of showering that night, I slept with the scent of the river, sun-dried on my skin and hair, puzzling over what had happened. Although Nan and I paddled our slow way upstream several times that summer after the encounter with the golden boy, I never saw him again. Sometimes I wonder if he ever even existed, or what would unfold within me if I could untangle the knot of memory that contains him, a knot tight as those in the rope swing the neighbor boys swung out from over the river.

Nan went off to boarding school at the end of the summer, while I entered North Salem High, and our lives flowed in different directions. I saw her sometimes, when she came home on school breaks, and even slept over at her house once or twice. We smoked our first joints together, and I remember consoling her over a hopeless crush on an undeserving boy. But things weren't the same. We never swam together in the pond again or went up the river, paddling to Connecticut. When I wanted to swim, I rode my bike seven miles to Lake Mamanasco, just over the state line, or snuck into Titicus Reservoir, where swimming was forbidden because it was part of the New York City water supply. But sometimes, during later summers, when my siblings and I hiked up Hunt Mountain at dusk, I'd gaze down at the Titicus River as it wound, silvery slow, through the fields far below. I'd think about Nan and wonder about the boy, who he was and where he'd come from. Did something of our conversation linger in the Titicus? Does the river remember what I have forgotten, as water is said to contain all conversations that happen beside it, and, if so, what would it tell me?

Several years ago, visiting North Salem for the first time in almost thirty years, I stood on the bridge at the end of the lane where I'd met the fisherman, looking down at the river and listening carefully, as if the girl I had been there could recount her story. But all I heard was the river as it echoed under the bridge, its reverberations rippling up through my body, familiar yet incomprehensible as they had been the first time I felt them. There was no voice there but that of the water itself, running on as it always had over the copper-colored stones, the spell of gravity pulling it forward and away from me, no matter how hard I tried to hold it.

VI. Day Lily: Interlude with Colonial House and Stream

The spring I was fifteen, the property where we lived in North Salem was put up for sale, for a sum far greater than anything my perpetually strapped parents could afford. We left the big white Georgian-style house, perched like a ship in full sail on the hill behind its white picket fence, and moved to the other end of the township, into another old house on 150 acres, part of it in Putnam County, which might as well have been another country, as far as I was concerned. The house, which my parents were lucky to find, had been built in 1753 and is the oldest I have ever lived in. Owned by an absentee landlord, who lived on Prince Edward Island (in what seemed to me romantic isolation), the house was beloved, but rented out because of some mysterious sadness his wife associated with the place. Long, low, and white, with green shutters and a porch that ran its entire front length, the house, as I would discover while writing a paper about it in college, merged two architectural styles—Dutch Colonial and New England saltbox. One entered through a massive oak door, many inches thick and held by iron hinges, its wood pocked here and there by holes the landlord claimed were made by Revolutionary War musket balls.

Stepping inside, we were in another century. The beams and rafters that held the house up were massive, hand hewn with an adze. The floors were wide oak planks, polished to a buttery sheen by the passage of time. A fieldstone fireplace dominated the living room, its chimney so big the steep stairs to the second floor unpleated up around it, accordion style. The hearth was a single, massive slab of stone, which we wondered about, marveling over how settlers could have maneuvered it there. Staring into the fire on cold winter nights, I tried to imagine what it must have been like to cook at that hearth, a pot dangling from the enormous iron hook that still hung above the flames like a soot-blackened claw.

I had lived in old houses before and would do so again. But I have never inhabited a house imbued with as deep a sense of previous inhabitants as the one on Field's Lane. My sister, my stepmother, and I all saw ghosts there. When I wrote the paper about the house for my American Art and Architecture class, I corresponded with the landlord's sad wife and learned something of its history, enough to corroborate that the ghosts we saw—one of mine was a young woman in an eighteenth-century dance dress—matched her descriptions of previous inhabitants. Thinking about ghosts, I wondered where my mother's was, and if she perhaps haunted Wild Run Farm, roaming its rooms, which stood empty for five years before the house sold. The sorrow our landlord's wife felt had opened a window briefly on my own.

It is impossible to live in a house as steeped in history as the one on Field's Lane was and not feel a sense of what John Hanson Mitchell calls "ceremonial time," that one is part of a continuum of lives that have passed before. Lying in bed at night, my resentment at having to share a room—the former side parlor—with my sister tempered by the fact that we had our own small fireplace, I'd muse about all that had happened in those low-ceilinged rooms, the house breathing around me. It had seen everything, and it took us in, protecting us, even as our family unraveled after my stepmother had an affair with my father's best friend in the pharmaceutical business. At times it seemed it was only the house that held us there, deep in the country, where the world still seemed safe. We rarely locked the front door except at night.

The house was marvelous, but what lay outside was even better. Rising steeply behind the house, the sunny meadow, where a neighbor's old horse grazed, transitioned quickly into woods of oak, beech, and sugar maple. Bisected by stone walls and rarely used bridle paths, this was a private realm, one that provided us kids with a refuge from the unhappy adults in our lives. We quickly claimed the woods as ours, establishing a rough camp in a clutch of conifers, which we called "the

Pine Forest," at the top of the hill. We spent many summer nights camped out under the stars, glad to be out of the house where our parents' arguments echoed down the heating vents. To get there, we had to cross the stream that ran behind the house. We referred to it, in the nomenclature of rural places everywhere, as "*the* Stream," as if there were no other. But because I secretly named it Day Lily, for the orange flowers that grew thickly along its banks, I will call it that here.

Day Lily Creek did not actually begin in the Pine Forest, but somewhere farther uphill, where a spring bubbled up from the ground. But it seemed to start in that place we'd made our own, spurting from between tumbled granite stones with a sound like many tiny, muted hoofbeats. Bouncing and sparkling, twisting and turning, Day Lily tore down the hill, until it slowed and wound sedately behind the house, at the edge of the terraced garden my father referred to as "the lower meadow." If, as Gretel Ehrlich has written, "a stream is an expression of its watershed; that is, liquid…literally 'expressed' from an ecological matrix, the green breast of Earth," it seems right that our stream began near the spot where we slept on so many evenings, at a sweet remove from the turmoil and trouble between our parents. Flowing as it did, between the yard and the woods, Day Lily marked a line between the world of home and the world where we kids were on our own, stepping through a forest which, though it was actually second growth hardwood, felt primeval.

We built a stone fire ring in the Pine Forest, around which we slept, rayed out around it like spokes in a wagon wheel. We had no proper equipment, no tents or sleeping bags, just blankets and pillows we'd pulled from our beds. Rolled up in my blue flowered quilt, I learned that, to get comfortable, I had to let my body relax into the ground, until I could feel what I thought of as the bones of the earth holding me in their hard embrace. But even then, I lay awake, listening to the stream's clear voice for a long time after my sister and brothers had fallen asleep. Had the Indians given a name to this creek? Had the ghost of the young woman I'd glimpsed in the house ever walked up here, listening to it as I did? Did Day Lily Creek recognize us kids as we arrived on summer evenings, a ragtag band of explorers and escapees, making our way through the dark to our place of refuge? The sound of running water filled my consciousness until I felt a part of it, glimmering there beside us in the night, like a black scarf shot with threads of silver, moonlight reflected on its wavering surface. Why did the murmur of the stream make me feel both full and lonely as I lay beside it?

I listened and listened, until discomfort gave way to fatigue and I slept. And though I've slept outside in many places since,

The Persistence of Rivers

I do not think I have ever slept as deeply as I did on those summer nights in the Pine Forest, my siblings and stepbrothers piled around me like puppies, the stream's shimmering and sibilant mystery carrying me into the darkness. In the morning, we woke, cranky and stiff, the magic of our night in the Pine Forest countered by the reality of having to return to the pain and confusion in our lives. Still, we were filled with the sense of having been some place special. Trooping back down the hill, we were strangely quiet, holding the sound of the stream and wind in the pines inside us, careful not to spill a drop.

The Pine Forest and the source of Day Lily were our escape and refuge. But the place where we interacted most frequently with the stream was where it curled around the lower meadow, then straightened out to run alongside the yard behind the house. I spent hours sitting next to it, trailing my fingers in the cool, clear water, watching water striders cast their four leaf clover-shaped shadows on the surface and sandy bottom, and daydreaming about a future I could hardly imagine, except that I knew it had to be better than the way I was living now. Sometimes Day Lily was a mute witness as I paced beside it, fuming, filled with adolescent storm and outrage about everything (from my stepmother insisting I wash the kitchen floor every day, to my being grounded for a month for having dared to cross her, to a teacher who had given me a detention for being a smart-ass in class), until the sound of running water brought me back to myself. But one spring morning, I glanced out the kitchen window to where the stream, full of rain and snowmelt, had overflowed its low banks, spreading across the yard in a shallow lake that reflected the house, perched on the rise, like a dinghy. We were never in danger and the water went down a day or two later, having revealed a fiercer face of our gentle companion. But it was disconcerting to realize that something so tranquil could become a force of destruction.

Nearly every afternoon after school, over endless cups of Constant Comment tea at the battered kitchen table with my sister, I'd glance up, noticing how her face, our hands, the room itself were held in the reflection of the stream's wavering light. *Don't ever forget this*, I thought, looking into her thick-lashed grey eyes, so like our mother's had been. I picked watercress in the stream, reveling in its sharp green scent, and I wept there when a cement mixer from the gravel pit down the road hit and killed one of our kittens. One blistering August afternoon, I burned a love letter to a boy and threw the charred bits into the clear water, watching them float under the bridge and away. I splashed Day Lily's cool water over me as I lay beside it, tanning myself with a home-made cardboard "reflector" covered with tin foil. Once I lay down in the stream full length in my home-made paisley bikini, letting the water wash gently around me, as if it could smooth out all my rough edges. It almost seemed that it did.

Apart from the tiny creek running into the Perkiomen near Wild Run Farm, Day Lily was the smallest thread of running water I had ever known. Intimate, familiar, and domestic (as the tumbledown springhouse across the road attested), the stream was so much a part of my daily landscape I sometimes barely even saw it. But it defined everything around it. I missed the sound of Day Lily when I was away at a friend's house overnight and had to imagine the sound of the water turning over itself, mixed with the breeze in the big maple outside my window, and the horses cropping hay and timothy in the field. One could cross Day Lily's narrowest places in a single running bound, but the three quick steps needed to get across the board bridge to the woods are still alive in my body, instinctive as breathing, familiar as home. The step in the middle, directly over the water, always sounded hollow, resonant with the possibility of falling in. I think I could pace it out perfectly even now, were I returned there, to the sound of the little stream shushing down its sandy channel—running I know not where, pulling me back into my life the way the future pulled me away—and to the house that echoed so richly, filled with history, possibility, and sadness. I left Day Lily behind when I left home for college. But the sound of its water runs within me yet, cold and pure as the springs that fed it.

VII. Marys River, Wren, Oregon

In the first story I ever wrote, when Mrs. Wilson allowed us to choose our own topic in third grade, I told the tale of a pioneer family, traveling by covered wagon on the Oregon Trail to what I described as "a deep green place of plenty, beside a silver river," a landscape I imagined as a kind of promised land. I was in my "pioneer phase," having torn through the Little House books the year before and moved on to titles like *Heroines of the Early West* and *The Oregon Trail*, which clearly influenced my literary efforts. But I have always wondered if that story, which Mrs. Wilson had me bind between green construction paper covers—decorated with an awkward-looking wagon—to hang on the bulletin board, wasn't mysteriously prescient, anticipating something I would only discover when I finally moved to Oregon in my thirties. From the minute our yellow Ryder rental van began descending out of Ashland toward the sun-bleached, green-gold that is the Willamette Valley in late summer, I felt as if I had found a real home, arriving, after a long journey, in the place where I truly belonged. Oregon lay before me, as I imagined it had before the pioneers.

The Persistence of Rivers

If we are lucky, there are landscapes in our lives that work on us as if we are part of the land itself, shaping us, scraping us, refining us, making us into more of who we really are. Some do this by imprinting us psychically, the way eastern Pennsylvania imprinted me, its clear rivers, fields, and hardwood forests so much a part of my inner geography that it became what nature writer Susan Shetterly describes as the "standard of comfort by which [I] measure whatever else is real in the world and whatever else is beautiful." Other landscapes work on us by being so different from anything we have ever known that they require us to create a whole new set of internal and external reference points. California, where I lived for over a decade in my twenties and early thirties, before moving to Oregon, had been like that for me. With its Mediterranean air, sharply etched mountains, and implacable sunlight, California demanded change. It knocked me down with its heat and vastness. It pummeled me with its backyard sea. It burnt me brown and limber as I hiked its foothills, the scent of sage and California bay laurel baking in sunlight an incense only possible in that place.

But still other landscapes shape us by being so familiar that they seem a country we have always known, a place we can step into and feel immediately part of, not native—that would presume too much—but accepted, as the shoots of lilac pioneer women brought west with them in their wagons were accepted by the Oregon soil. When I moved to Oregon, I felt as if I knew where I was. It was not so much that I recognized something in the landscape (though it was, indeed, beautiful to me), as that I felt welcomed by it, taken in. Bounded on one side by the Cascades and on the other by the Coast Range, the Willamette Valley in western Oregon is like an enormous, slightly cupped hand, one that holds its residents as gently as Mrs. Wilson had held my hand, her fingers around mine as we pinned my story on the bulletin board. This was earth I could grow in, a place where I could imagine sinking my roots deep and staying forever, which is, perhaps, the dream of every pioneer.

At first, I was only aware of this subliminally. I was broken when I came to Oregon and the Marys River, which rushes, like a wide silver path, twisting and turning from its headwaters in the Coast Range toward the Willamette, which in turn flows north, toward the Columbia and the Pacific. It was 1986, and my first husband, David, and I had moved to Oregon so he could take a position at Oregon State University. Several months before our move, I'd had a nervous breakdown and been hospitalized for two weeks. "Major Depression, Single Episode" was what it said on my medical chart, packed somewhere deep in that yellow moving van. But I knew depression had been with me my entire life, the blue fingerprint of something deeper and more terrible than ordinary sadness pressed firmly into my being after my mother's too-early death. Winston Churchchill, who suffered from depression, too, famously described it as his "black dog." I only wished my depression, which had risen up within me like an insidious fog, blurring my ability to think, to read, even to eat, and making me feel detached from everything—the clinical term is "depersonalized"—could be given as tangible a label.

I had been cracked into pieces. But I arrived in Oregon tentatively reassembled. Through a combination of medication, therapy, and exercise, plus my own ferocious desire to heal, I had pulled myself together enough that, at least on the surface, I seemed to be who I had been before. Two weeks after I got out of the hospital, our decade-long bond cemented by what we had gone through together, David and I were married under the palm trees in our backyard. A week later, we'd packed the van and headed nearly a thousand miles north with our three cats. "We're going to the promised land," I joked, as we chugged up I-5, through California's blistering Central Valley. But I was only partly kidding. After what I had experienced, Oregon did seem a promised land, a place where I might begin again, the way the pioneers had, making a new life, and reclaiming the more confident self I felt I had lost along the way.

Because my illness delayed our move, we arrived in Corvallis ("heart of the valley") without housing. Although we'd originally planned to live in town, an ad about a place for rent on seven acres along the Marys River, twelve miles west of town, at the edge of the Coast Range, piqued our interest. And so we found ourselves heading west on Highway 20, toward the coast. Just before the road began to rise seriously, darkening into a winding green tunnel shadowed by fir trees, we turned north on the King's Valley Highway, crossed the bridge over Marys River and turned left. In minutes, we were walking around the property at Priest Road.

I still remember the sense of having stumbled into an enchanted realm that fell over us as we got out of the car. A mix of oak savanna, Douglas fir, Noble fir, and open pasture land, the property was bounded on one side by the Marys River and on the other by the quiet road, which was supposedly named for the pioneer family who'd settled the land and from whose ancestors we would be renting the house. From the beginning, it was the land that claimed our attention. The house, painted a pale green, was nondescript and its best features were views of the mountains and a wide back deck facing the river. But the land took us in and seemed to hold us in a way I had not been held in a very long time. California had taught me a lot about the West, but I sensed Oregon would take me deeper. I took a deep breath and exhaled slowly. Standing there, in that narrow valley, bounded on three sides by mountain foothills and cut through by the river, trying to absorb the many variations of green, I felt as if I had been tucked safely inside a pocket lined with emerald moss.

No one seemed to be about, but David and I stepped hesitantly around the property. Stone-edged flower beds filled with bush fuchsias and roses were scattered through the backyard. There was a small pond, where I'd watch the delicate, aqueous dance of rough-skinned newts mating the following spring. A grape arbor bearing five kinds of grapes ran the width of the property, down to the river. Blackberry brambles lifted their lanterns of purple fruit everywhere. Marys Peak, the highest mountain in the Coast Range, floated, just to the south of us, like a humpback whale, gauzy clouds trailing behind it like torn chiffon scarves. Wind sighed through the fir trees, green spires that would imprint their shape upon me, altering my frame of reference so that ever after, when out walking, I would look up automatically, searching for their conical shape and the shape of the mountains behind them. The sound of the river, which bore my mother's name and was visible through the trees along the bank, ran through everything, its liquid burble and thrum like a mother's heartbeat. After having lived, as I had, for many years in a desert place, the river sounded like a voice I had once known well but had not heard for a very long time. I recognized it immediately, as I have always believed I might recognize my mother's voice were I ever to hear it aloud again. The river called out to me, taking me back to my beginnings beside the Perkiomen.

The house was empty, but the caretaker had been there, watering the yard. He had gone home for lunch, leaving on Rainbird sprinklers that hissed here and there, spangling everything with what we'd later learn was water pumped directly from the river. It flicked across us, wetting our faces, soothing us with its cold sweetness. "It seems too good to be true," David said, turning toward me, weeks of tension draining from his face. "Yes," I replied, feeling the same sense of relief. "I think we should take it." And so we did, moving into the little green house along the river on the land that matched so closely what I had imagined in my childhood story.

What is it that makes us fall in love with a landscape? What makes a place a home, even if it is, like the acreage along the Marys River in the unincorporated hamlet called Wren was for me, somewhere we have never been before? How do certain places align themselves so profoundly with something in our spirit they exert an almost physical pull upon us? A poet, not a geographer, I can only speculate, agreeing with Barry Lopez, who says certain "landscapes... [ease] a particular kind of longing." Although I had grown to love California during my years there, even taking pride in being a kind of latter day California Girl, on some level the Golden State had always been a place of temporary sojourn. Like so many other people, I had reinvented myself there, finding my voice in writing, discovering who I really was. But home? That was a different story. Home was wetter, softer, greener, infused with what, after having lived in Oregon for a while, I joked was the ancestral British-Celtic pull of ocean and rain. I had not thought about the fact it also meant living beside a river so like the one I had known as a child.

I did not yet know, on the afternoon we looked at the property, that the Kalapuya Indian name for Marys Peak, Tcha Teemanwi (pronounced tcha-TEE-man-wee), meant "Place Where Spirits Dwell," or that they sent their adolescent boys and girls to the mountain on vision quests to hear the voices and stories of their guardian spirits. I did not know the stories that said the river was named for the first white woman who crossed it in the early 1850s. I did not know the names of common things—twinberry, snowberry, Oregon lilies, salal—I would come to love, learning the lexicon of that place to express what I hadn't known before. I knew only the river had my mother's name and that something about the spot was so deeply comforting I never wanted to leave it. Perhaps it is enough to say it eased my longing. Perhaps it is enough to say I sensed in the land itself a kind of awareness or attention I wanted to make my own. Perhaps "where we are interacts reciprocally with who we are," as poet Reg Saner says, making us into something different and bigger. Perhaps the river called me home.

Following the grape arbor down to the river that first day, I came to a break in the undergrowth, a natural sitting spot next to a wide shelf of rock, shaped like the Indian head on old nickels. I stepped out on the rock and stood, surrounded by water on three sides. The river was wide and shallow here, its bed a cobble of perfectly arranged amber stones. Green-gold light filtered through firs and alders, dappling the surface of the water as it spilled downriver toward the bridge, beneath which cliff swallows flitted to and from their nests, slicing the air with their blue flight. Hunkering down on the rock, I dipped my hands spontaneously into the river, lifting the water and spilling it over my face. It smelled of moss and stones and time. Even as it evaporated, I felt as if it blessed me, washing through me, welcoming me to the place.

And I needed that welcome. Although I looked—and in many ways was—well again, with the tricyclic antidepressant nortriptyline playing its serotonin trick on my synapses, the brokenness of the experience went deeper than even I knew. I was functioning, but my connection to what I called the "normal" world felt tenuous. I watched myself unpack boxes from our move, place dishes in cupboards, hang pictures, take walks, follow the river. Many days I felt as if all that held me to the earth were the fragile ropes of my new routine, part of which involved giving myself over to the natural world in a way I hadn't since I was a child. After writing—or attempting to write—in the morning, I'd go out for a long run, then come down to the river and sit on the Indian rock for a long time, staring into the water as it flowed past. Sitting so still I felt a part of the landscape, I gave myself over to observation. I watched as a doe and her fawn bent their graceful heads to drink, studied the slow fan of a blue heron unfurling its wings, stared into a pool filled with minnows the length of my little finger, followed a steelhead as it finned its way upstream. Everything was holy; everything required my attention. The act of looking took me outside myself and my own obsessive concerns, filling me up with the world around me until there was no room for my problems. If I contemplated the river long enough, I became the river.

Alison Townsend

If I was having an especially shaky day—and there were more of those than I would have liked—I engaged in a practice I called river walking, which involved stepping slowly upstream through the water, moving against the current. Although there was a swimming hole downriver, on the other side of the bridge, where the water was over my head, the river was broad and flat where it ran along our property, never more than waist deep. One day, having waded into the river to cool down after running, I was struck by the way the water first touched my body and then parted around me, as if I were as solid as rock or snag. And so I began walking through water. Something about the ritual soothed me, as if the pulse of the current against my body washed all fear and anxiety away, dissolving it, sending it downstream and away, into something larger. I'd wade upstream for what seemed like hours, caressed by the river's invisible hands, moving through a constantly shifting reflection of the alders and fir trees that grew along the banks and my own body that blurred then grew still behind me, until I felt steady enough to go back into the house again.

From the beginning of my time beside it, I understood the river had things to tell me. But it offered comfort in ways that had nothing to do with language, which was part of what made it so healing. Whether I was sitting on my Indian rock, still as the deer I watched drinking there, wading across glinting pebbles flecked with mica, or swimming in water the color of honey, the river held me in an embrace that was both soothing and indifferent to my human struggle. No matter what I did, the river flowed around me, its ceaseless, sibilant conversation washing me as clear as water itself. It was a time without words that led me slowly back to words, a mysterious parallel to my early childhood beside the Perkiomen, when all I'd heard for hours was the sound of the water talking to itself as it slipped silkily over stones. Listening to the water, I imagined I could hear the voices of pioneer women and children who once lived on its banks, tilling gardens, washing clothes, tending animals. I was aware, too, of pools of silence that had fallen into the water miles away, traveling toward me like small oases of calm that held me. I gave myself up to them and they eased my sadness. And always the river purled along, deeply familiar, but at the same time constantly changing, never the same from one day to the next.

When the rains began in the early fall, I watched as they filled the river and were swept away, as it seemed my own tears were. Though logic suggests the wet Pacific Northwest winter with its long, silver-grey days might be hard for a depressive, it wasn't like that for me. I felt invigorated and rejuvenated by rain. I loved learning its many varieties, its subtle language, and how it came and went, now a deluge, now a sparkling beaded curtain, now diaphanous, sun-shot mist. Most of all, I loved running in it, my legs pink with cold, my yellow, Moosehead beer t-shirt soaked to the skin, logging trucks honking as they barreled past when I turned on to Highway 20. I loved the feeling of rain upon my face and how it licked me gently, everywhere, like a thousand tiny tongues.

One spring, when the river ran high in its banks and spilled over into the lower yard, creating an extended, shallow pool, I felt a little afraid, watching as it churned, dense as muddy coffee, filled with froth and broken branches. It wasn't the friendly, sun-dappled river of summer then and seemed dangerous, capable of sweeping me away, the way anxiety sometimes did. But the waters receded, and the next summer, David and I bought an inflatable yellow raft, in which we explored areas downstream, expanding our understanding of the river. As I got to know the area, running and riding my bike, I found a place nearby where a covered bridge like the one from my childhood spanned the river. When my father visited, I took a picture of him before the bridge, tucking it into an old scrapbook next to a deckle-edged snapshot of him standing beside the bridge over the Perkiomen, holding me as a baby. Always the river was familiar, its sound taking me back to my origins beside water, beginning me again. Like the wild foxgloves that bloomed in pink spires everywhere, reappearing every year, perennial, I wanted to stay there forever.

We knew when we moved to Oregon that our time there was limited. David's salary was paid for with a grant from the Environmental Protection Agency, due to run out in a couple of years, possibly renewable but with no promises. But life in the beneficent Oregon landscape beside the Marys River was so healing for me that I could not imagine leaving and forced any thoughts of doing so into the background. I found a writing group and began teaching at both the local community college and through a community education program. I began to find my way and built a small, local reputation for my women's writing workshops. One wild March day, as I walked around the back yard, cooling down from a four-mile run, the blackout window blind of depression rolled up in my head with a sharp snap and the world, indeed my entire being, seemed flooded with light. I was myself again, back from the underworld I had stumbled into two years before. I fell to my knees and, kneeling there, among primroses and mud, I gave thanks, watching as Marys Peak sailed through the clouds, the sound of the river running through everything. Did my soul somehow know my time at Marys River was running out, that I needed to be completely well to carry on?

David's funding wasn't extended. I would have done anything to stay and lined up more teaching and work in the local independent bookstore. But David was unable and unwilling to jettison a nascent academic career. He liked Oregon, but it didn't mean the same thing to him that it did to me. We began making plans to move, following yet another job, this time to Denver. It was the beginning of the end of us, though neither of us saw it at the time. I knew only that I was leaving something that felt so much a part of me and so crucial to my well being I was not sure I would survive without it. In the months before we moved, I dreamed my flowerbeds were uprooted, Marys Peak disappeared, and the river itself overflowed, washing the little green house away.

The day we left Oregon, I ran around the backyard, taking photographs, while David waited impatiently in the truck, the cats' carriers piled high on the seat beside him. Afraid I might forget something, I snapped random glimpses of it all—the mossy oaks, the grape arbor, the fir trees, the mountain, and the river, glinting that day like broken silver between the trees. Every leave-taking I had ever experienced seemed conflated into this one, and I felt frantic, panic stricken, as if, like a small child, I might have to be physically pried away from the place, kicking and screaming. The last thing I did was go down to my Indian rock and stand there, the water swirling past, all rill and stillness. I could hardly bear the idea that it was all going to go on without me, and yet of course, it would. I belonged to the river, but the river wasn't mine. I thought again about the folk beliefs that rivers remember every voice they have ever heard. I knelt and splashed my face with water as I had that first day. *Remember me*, I said softly, dropping my voice into the river with all the others it carried. Then I turned and walked away, as I had from so many other places. My heart was broken over leaving, but I was stronger from my time there.

Over a quarter of a century away from my departure, having learned with difficulty to love another place, I still cannot look at the pictures I took that day. I know the river lives on within me, the persistence of water in my life the source of memory, recovery, and dream. But that is not the same as living beside it, and I have never completely reconciled myself to its absence. The Marys River taught me to again regard the world the way a child does, crouched down and staring, alive to every swirl and reflection. The river taught me to move as it did, letting the simple pull of the current hold me as I returned to myself, one shining rib of light at a time. Where the river meandered and slowed in stands of camas and cattails, it taught me to relax, merging with "the line of beauty" Thoreau says dwells "in the curve." Most of all, it brought me to a place of healing, which, though on the other side of the country from the place where I began, so closely echoed my beginnings beside the Perkiomen that it seemed my whole life was contained there, a channel carved deeply between bright green banks. Perhaps I would not know any of these things had I never left it. Or perhaps I would know them more deeply and truly, now a "semi-native" Oregonian the green t-shirt I bought proclaimed I was. I cannot say. All I know is this: I left the river, but it has not left me. Like water, which is restless even when contained, I am still searching for my level.

VIII. *The Yahara River, Pleasant Springs Township, Wisconsin*

It's been many years since I've lived with a river running through my backyard, decades since the claims of love and work took me from the Marys River. Where I live now, on the north side of a drumlin in the rolling farm country outside Madison, Wisconsin, I look down over Island Lake, a spring-fed, glacier-sculpted beauty that shimmers among the fields, reflecting every change of light and weather. The lake, with its bristly, oak-covered island, is a focal point, and restful to the eye. It has become a kind of spiritual compass for me, a place where I daily take my bearings. The waters of Island Lake are a constant backdrop, shining among the cattail marshes like time's own mirror.

I love the constancy of the lake, but I miss the sense of possibility offered by moving water. Lakes invite contemplation and inner stillness. Rivers, while mesmerizing and hypnotic, are mutable, one thing forever becoming another as the water slides past, always on its way somewhere else. As Oregon writer John Daniel notes, "We don't tend to ask where a lake comes from. It lies before us, contained and complete, tantalizing in its depth but not in its origin.... A river," he speculates, "is a different kind of mystery, a mystery of distance and becoming, a mystery of source."

I'm not sure I agree that lakes, especially spring-fed ones like mine, don't tantalize us with their origins. Springs are, after all, mysteries of their own, bubbling up from earth as they do, and the lake has its own magic. But I think Daniel captures an essential truth about rivers when he says they are each "[mysteries] of distance and becoming." For what do rivers speak to in us but our own insatiable curiosity? Curiosity about what comes next, what lies around the curve, what kind of fish or bird or animal or aquatic insect the next riffle might reveal. *Where has the river come from?* we wonder. And where will it take us if we surrender to its currents, savoring how it reveals itself to us by taking us somewhere, showing us to ourselves as we ride its silver back, the river in endless motion and evolution, just like us?

These days, when I spend time beside a river, the one that companions me is the Yahara, within whose watershed I reside. Named after the Ho-Chunk word for "catfish," the Yahara originates north of Madison and flows through the area's famous chain of four lakes—Mendota, Monona, Waubesa, and finally, windy Kegonsa, which lies closest to where I live. From here, the Yahara heads south, toward its confluence with the Rock River (along which my Wisconsin-born husband

Tom spent his boyhood), which in turn joins the Mississippi, flowing on, like all rivers, toward the sea.

Tom and I have canoed nearly all of the Yahara and love especially a winding, wooded section south of where we live. Here I have learned the difference between canoeing on rivers and on lakes. Here I have learned to paddle in tandem with my husband, so that sometimes it seems we and his yellow canoe, "Good Medicine," are one being. Here I have heard the raspy *skyew* of a startled green heron, and held my breath as we watched a deer drinking, her brown eyes reflecting the river's wild wisdom as we slipped silently past.

A still-ambivalent transplant to Wisconsin, I am surprised to realize that I have spent more time canoeing the Yahara than any other river. How did this come to be? And what has this apparently unprepossessing river taught me when I wasn't aware of anything but the pleasure of motion upon its waters, my paddle lifted, dripping with water weeds and gilded by sunlight? Like the river, I realize I have been in motion the whole time, my life running with a power and momentum I only sometimes understand, each of us a mystery to ourselves, after all, until the moment of final reckoning. "Shall we gather at the river?" the old hymn asks. Perhaps that is when I will grasp what rivers mean.

The Persistence of Rivers

Certain moments canoeing on the Yahara stand out in my mind, like the bright beads of rain I once saw, strung on a storm-drenched spider web spun on a fallen tree, or the row of basking painted turtles I glimpsed, lined up on a log in the sun, their shells shining like polished enamel boxes. But most of my time with this river has been spent on foot, strolling beside it at the local dog park, as my two tri-colored collies lope ahead. There's a play area for water-loving dogs, who fling themselves with abandon off the dock built for this purpose, chasing sticks and balls (an activity I am secretly glad my dogs disdain). But mostly the river serves as a kind of liquid fence, keeping dogs safely on the isthmus of the park. I walk beside the water, measuring my steps to its cadence, listening again for voices I might recognize; the water, as always, speaking a language it seems I once knew.

As I walk, I am seduced by the Yahara's cattail marshes and sedge meadows, its sandhill cranes and snowy egrets, its kingfishers and great blue herons, its ever-present flocks of honking Canada geese. I watch the way tree swallows dip over the water, the blue-green sheen of their wings like delicate scissors cutting a path through the air, and admire hoards of red-winged blackbirds as they twist and turn in complex skeins, their voices a thousand creaky screen doors flung open on spring. The Yahara is neither as beautiful nor as beloved to me as rivers I've known in the past. Often a soupy gray-green in high summer, clouded with algae, whose growth is encouraged by the agricultural run-off endemic to this part of the Upper Midwest, it's not always appealing. In winter, whether frozen over or clogged with dragons' teeth of broken ice, it's grey and foreboding. But there are times when, standing on a sheltered, half-moon beach where the water moves more slowly, I can see right through to the river's sandy bottom, reminded that nothing stays the same. Everything—the river, life, me—changes. And after that, it changes again.

I love the way the Yahara links—and makes possible—the four big lakes, running like a silvery umbilicus between them. I love how it swallows the sky, so that, walking beside it, I almost lose perspective—the reflections of oaks in the water as real as the trees they mirror—and feel I am walking on clouds. I love the way the river pushes against its few small dams and am happy one of them has been taken down, allowing the water its natural momentum. Most of all, I love the way the river seems to dream in early October, its deeper currents hidden beneath its apparently still face. Staring into the water, I almost grasp something in the mystery in all rivers. Simultaneously here and there, behind and ahead, moving and calm, rivers take me deep into my own past and beyond the present, into an unknown future.

The Persistence of Rivers

Once, standing alone on the small, sandy beach, I had the urge to dip my hands in the water. Cupping my palms, I was startled to see my own lifeline, sharply visible in a way I hadn't noticed before, glimmering up at me even as the water slipped between my fingers. Was my life a river, too? Despite all my years watching rivers, it was a story I hadn't thought to tell myself before. If, as Ursula Le Guin says, "[s]tory is our only boat for sailing the river of time," this moment was one of my tales, a liquid page scripted by ripples, eddies, and whorls of water.

Which is perhaps the rivers' greatest mystery and what keeps me coming back to them, despite my love of mountains and oceans. I am caught and held by rivers, pushed and pulled by them, sung into being by their very river-ness, as incapable of resisting their flow as I am of not breathing. Each river I encounter changes me, baptizing me with its wildness into who I am at the moment—a source, a channel, a pair of grassy banks, a flood—allowing me the promise of rebirth as surely as if I have been hallowed by total immersion. As sometimes I am, gathered with my many selves beside the river of *then* and *now*, listening and watching for what comes next, my life remade by moving water as it quickens, gathers, and falls, rushing always toward the next bend, around which the shining path seems to go on forever.

Acknowledgements

My parents understood the importance of wild places and rivers; this book is informed by their memory and spirit. I am grateful to my writing group, The Lake Effect Poets, for allowing me to impose nonfiction upon them and for responding with perceptive commentary. Marilyn Annucci, Catherine Jagoe, and Judith Sornberger have been vital essayist friends, unfailingly honest, insightful, and wise in their counsel. My husband, Tom Umhoefer, has not only read and re-read these pages, but has taken me down rivers I might otherwise have never explored; this book is for him. Special thanks to Jennifer Worsley, for art that makes the soul of rivers visible, and to Liesl Swogger for the elegant cover and book design. Deepest gratitude to Susan Fallows and Lisa Roney of *The Florida Review*, to contest judge Vanessa Blakeslee, and to Ryan Rivas of Burrow Press for their editing, vision, generosity, and support in making this book what it is. One couldn't ask for a better team.

About the Author

Alison Townsend is the author of two books of poetry, *The Blue Dress: Poems and Prose Poems*, and *Persephone in America*, as well as two poetry chapbooks, *And Still the Music*, and *What the Body Knows*. Her writing has won a Pushcart Prize, The Crab Orchard Open Poetry Competition, a Wisconsin Literary Arts Grant, and many other awards. Her poetry has appeared in numerous journals and has been anthologized in *Best American Poetry 2006* and *2010 Pushcart Prize*. Her essays have appeared in *Brevity*, *Chautauqua*, *Parabola*, *The Southern Review*, and *Zone 3*, among others, and have been listed as notable in *Best American Essays 2014*, *2015*, and *2016* and received special mention in the *2017 Pushcart Prize*. Professor Emerita of English and Women's Studies at the University of Wisconsin-Whitewater, she lives in the farm country outside Madison.

About the Cover Artist

Jennifer Worsley studied painting and drawing at The New York Academy of Art and Boston University. She now works on location in pastel, considering it the perfect medium for quickly capturing fleeting effects of light and weather. She says, "What interests me in an image is a sense of movement and, by implication, the passage of time. I am inspired by the challenge of capturing this fundamental aspect of nature."

The Florida Review

The Florida Review is the literary journal published twice yearly by the University of Central Florida. Its artistic mission is to publish the best poetry and prose written by the world's most exciting emerging and established writers. The journal has featured fiction, essays, poetry, and interviews with many notable authors, including David Foster Wallace, Margaret Atwood, Lorrie Moore, Stephen Graham Jones, Gerald Vizenor and Denise Duhamel. For more information about the Jeanne Leiby Award and *The Florida Review*, please visit floridareview.cah.ucf.edu.

Burrow Press

BP thrives on the direct support of enthusiastic readers like you. Your generous support has helped Burrow, since our founding in 2010, provide over 1,000 opportunities for writers to publish and share their work. We publish four, carefully selected books each year, offered in an annual subscription package. Subscriber contributions directly fund and sustain our publishing program. Learn more at: burrowpress.com/subscribe.

CPSIA information can be obtained
at www.ICGtesting.com
Printed in the USA
LVHW082042191119
637872LV00013B/1548/P